Paris in Oakland

Eliza Q Hemenway

ISBN-10: 1519578512
ISBN-13: 978-1519578518

For my daughter
Katherine

The following is a true story,
only names have been changed for privacy.

Paris in Oakland

ONE

*"For those who believe in God, no explanation is
necessary. For those who do not believe in God, no
explanation is possible."* -The Song of Bernadette

My head hit the back of the passenger seat as I
looked at the dark morning sky through slotted eyes. My
daughter lay in the back of the ambulance surrounded by
specialists in case one of her organs began shutting
down on the ride from Santa Rosa to Oakland. It usually
took over an hour's drive through bumper-to-bumper
traffic, but at three in the morning we sailed through
lanes of empty freeway.

Crossing the Richmond Bridge, I was struck by the
beauty of the ships alight in the bay as San Francisco
glimmered in the distance, the moon reflecting on the
water. The world was not going to stop whether my
daughter lived or died.

On a college road trip with friends, passing the
outskirts of Denver, I remember seeing rows of colorful
houses with porches and yards. I imagined myself living
in one of them, a daughter in a yellow sundress and
cowgirl boots running with a dog at her side, as I sat on
my porch drinking cool lemonade in the heat of summer.

Years later, I would move to Sebastopol, a small
town in Northern California, into a yellow farmhouse
with a great big porch and a little girl who wore

sundresses and ran in the back yard, a long mane of brown hair trailing behind. We had two dogs and an oak tree with a tire swing I could see from the kitchen window. I enrolled Katherine in a local school that boasted a redwood forest as its playground and every day she would make fairy houses under the giant trees and run through fields of tall grass. The kids planted sunflowers in the school garden and later ate seeds out of the towering golden flowers.

I thought I was giving my daughter an idyllic childhood in the country. Little did I know that under the leaf litter, hidden in the tall grass, somewhere in the redwood grove, could be the cause of so much suffering and would ultimately lead us to the 10th floor of Kaiser's Oakland Hospital.

+ + +

It took nearly eight years before we got the diagnosis of Lyme disease. By that time her illness was so advanced it was debilitating. First came the foot pain so severe she could barely keep up with the other children in gym class. Her teacher, thinking she was stubborn, hurled insults at Katherine and called her the most out of shape child she had ever taught. Then came the daily headaches, the stomachaches and later, the joint pain. Every year her symptoms grew worse and new ones developed. She missed more and more school. Extracurricular activities faded into the background, friends drifted away until all she could do was just make it through a school day, complete her homework, and fall into bed exhausted, in constant pain.

+ + +

The paramedics escorted us in a service elevator up to the 10th floor. I took in my surroundings, an old, dilapidated hospital. I could see part of the wall where it met the floor crumbling, wires exposed. I prayed for courage, strength and no fear. Normally I hated going up elevators into tall buildings. I imagined earthquakes, fires and every other possible disaster. Here, there was no choice. We were going up and in every way had to trust in the grace and sufficiency of God.

We arrived in the children's ward and were brought into the PICU, the Pediatric Intensive Care Unit. Curtains separated beds where children connected to tubes lay sleeping. Their parents lay next to them in chair beds. The noise was constant and I wondered how anyone could rest there. Seeming to read my thoughts, the attending nurse said, "When you get exhausted enough, you'll sleep." She went off to get linens, but before she could return, I pulled the chair out so it lay flat and curled up inches from my daughter's hospital bed. The next thing I knew it was morning.

A familiar face was standing over me. It was Beth from church. Her husband had been my daughter's youth pastor. Her little girl, Lilly, had been in the PICU for a couple of weeks and counting. She handed me a cup of strong, hot coffee with a big smile and in that moment a peace settled over me. I knew God was with us, even in that dreaded place.

Riding over in the ambulance the night before, the thought passed through my mind, "How will I get through this on hospital coffee?" It was no small thing; it was the creature comfort I needed most. Beth had brought the good stuff from a nearby café. Her standing there with that hot cup of coffee felt like Jesus' hands extended before me. It was more than a cup of coffee. It was a nod from God, "I am with you in this."

"And if anyone gives even a cup of cold water to one of these little ones who is my disciple, truly I tell you, that

7

person will certainly not lose their reward."
(Matthew 10:42)

That hot coffee was like cold water to my soul.

Beth wasted no time. Katherine was sleeping and her little Lilly was getting ready for breakfast. We had a short window and she was going to show me around and give me a tour of the 10th floor. I followed her out the PICU doors to where they kept the towels and linens, and around the corner to the one bathroom for all the parents to share. She told me what time was best to shower, before the morning rush, where to find things like plastic spoons and when they put out the plate of fresh fruit for parents. Next stop, Lilly's room. We arrived just as a tray of breakfast was being delivered. Beth plucked up her yogurt and handed it to me, "You'll need this." Later she told me where I could go for oatmeal and the much needed strong coffee. I was a mess. She was pulled together as if going to church on Sunday morning, hair done, impeccable makeup, neat, clean clothes. "When you've been here awhile you pull yourself together," she said. She had done a good job of it. Lilly beamed up at me with a smile that stretched from the east coast to the west. Her dad sat next to her bed looking tired. "Hi Matt," I said. This was not a place any two parents wanted to meet.

I made my way back to Katherine's room. I did not want to be gone when she woke up and soon the rounds would come. A swarm of doctors and nurses and various other people wearing white coats came by. It was all a fog as questions were asked and answered. It had not sunk in yet, how serious it had been, and apparently still was.

+ + +

"You know depression isn't just wanting to kill yourself," her pediatrician said. Katherine was ten years old. We had switched doctors three times already and as soon as the words came out of her mouth I knew it was time to change again. She had gotten annoyed with me during that appointment when I asked if Katherine's foot pain could be related to her headaches and other symptoms. It was all one body. "Surely it must be connected," I wondered aloud.

"The feet have nothing to do with the rest of the body. Your daughter is depressed," her doctor snapped at me. But she did not act depressed. She was in pain. There was a difference. I worried that if her doctor kept telling Katherine she was depressed, maybe she would start believing it. She began asking her friends and people close to her if they thought she was depressed. Nobody did. We needed a new doctor.

+ + +

The hospital doctors had made their rounds and the nurses had come and gone. I did not want to leave Katherine's side as she drifted in and out of consciousness. My friend Marge texted. She was dropping her husband off at the Oakland Airport later that day and would come by with sandwiches.

There was a moment of quiet and I decided to take advantage and try to get some rest. I lay back on the chair bed and just as I did, on the other side of the curtain, inches from my head, I overheard a nurse trying to comfort a young girl, "Don't cry." She had swelling on the brain and they needed to give her a lumbar puncture.

+ + +

By the time Katherine was in middle school I was getting calls three or four times a week to pick her up because she was too sick to finish the day. We had to make special arrangements for a reduced school schedule. Katherine missed almost every field trip, had to quit dance lessons, the school play and the swim team. Once a strong swimmer, she was now in too much pain to complete even one lap. Whatever was wrong with her was getting worse and we were getting nowhere with her doctors at Kaiser. It felt like we were caught in a great medical maze as we were bounced from one specialist to another, each one pointing us in different directions.

By the eighth grade she started having heart problems. I first noticed it at the gym. Her feet hurt too much to walk, and every time we tried to bike or swim, she had joint pain. I tried to get her to the gym for more controlled exercise. We were side by side on the elliptical machine, having just started our workout, when I noticed Katherine's heart rate read 172 beats per minute. Mine had not even hit 120 and I was working harder than she was. I thought something was wrong with the heart monitor on the machine, so I took her to the treadmill. The same thing happened. We came back again the next day, and once again, within minutes, her heart rate spiked. Whatever this was, it was now affecting her heart, and my momma-tiger-bear instincts were kicking in.

Her doctor seemed confused and kept insisting that I just needed to workout harder to catch up with Katherine. "No, you don't understand, we had just started exercising when her heart rate spiked," I tried explaining, "and then the dizziness and nausea set in." The polite term for fighting is advocating, and I had my work cut out for me. A pattern was emerging. Whatever symptoms I told her doctors, they minimized, dismissed and then denied care. This was not going to be dismissed. It was my daughter's heart. I insisted, "She needs to see a cardiologist."

Katherine was put on the treadmill for a stress test. "Alarming," the cardiologist called out to his assistant, "Stop the machine." It was happening again. Her heart rate was spiking with minimal activity and he was clearly concerned. He wrote down a word on a piece of paper and slipped it to me, "dysautonomia."

"What is that?" I asked, trying to figure out how to pronounce it.

"Go home and Google it, see what you find out and come back to me with any questions," he said. That was it. We left with this strange word written on a slip of paper. "But at least it's a direction," I thought, hopeful we would finally get answers to her ongoing health problems.

I typed "dysautonomia" into the computer. I had never heard of it before. It turned out it has to do with how the brain regulates the autonomic nervous center, such as heart rate. There seemed to be three possible causes: viral, Lyme disease, or a rare genetic disorder. This had been going on for so long. I assumed a virus would have been short lived, and the rare genetic disease seemed less likely, though possible. Lyme disease caught my attention. As I started to research it, the symptoms read like my daughter's medical history.

Lyme disease made sense. And in my mind, a diagnosis meant treatment and her health restored. I wasted no time emailing her doctor asking about Lyme disease. Her response was she was dropping Katherine from her panel. I did not even know doctors could do that and right when we were on the brink of answers. This was the worst time to start over with yet another doctor. I pleaded with her to stay with us. She responded that her panel was too full for a case as complex as ours, and just like that, we were without a doctor. After years of searching for a diagnosis, we now had to put it all on hold as we found a new primary doctor who would take a case with as complex a medical history as Katherine's, a case on the brink of a Lyme disease diagnosis.

TWO

As I drove through Sebastopol I kept seeing signs for a support group, "Tick Talk." I decided to call, thinking it might be a good resource, but by the end of the conversation I was so filled with fear and confusion I could not sleep for days. A woman answered the phone who had Lyme disease twice, "I only walk on pavement now," she told me. She seemed obsessed with the injustices of Lyme disease, "Don't trust anything the CDC says."

"Who's the CDC?" I asked.

"The Center for Disease Control," and she went on to rattle off a list of Lyme terms. I felt like I was learning a new language. I could barely keep up. "You need to get your girl to a Lyme-literate doctor."

"A who? A what?" I thought. Two hours later, I hung up the phone in shock.

+ + +

A nagging memory seemed to come out of nowhere and would not let go--a rash. I had a distant memory of a rash. When Katherine was seven years old. I thought it was ringworm at the time. It was a perfect circle. I was not even sure if this memory was real. I began to question myself, "Did she really have the rash," or was I just grasping for answers? I tried to shake it, but the memory just came back stronger. I started waking up in the middle of the night, bolting upright, remembering the rash. The prompting was so strong. I needed to go look into this rash and see if it was real.

I drove to Kaiser and marched into member services. Nobody was there except a secretary who reluctantly opened Katherine's file and began to search her records. "I really shouldn't be doing this," she kept saying.

"Why not?" I thought. It was my daughter's medical records. It was years of doctors visits and specialists, and would be like finding a needle in a haystack. As she was scrolling through her files I started to pray.

"I found it," she said moments later. There it was. Around the same time Katherine's symptoms began, she had a rash, a circular rash, a bull's-eye. The bull's-eye rash is one of the telltale signs of Lyme disease.

She had the rash when she was seven years old. It had been dismissed at the time; her doctor had assured me it was not ringworm. It went away and I had not thought about it again until recently. I asked the secretary to print out the record, but now she seemed agitated. She was visibly nervous. She hastily wrote down the date on a piece of paper and slipped it to me again saying, "I really shouldn't be doing this," and sent me to the medical records office. I felt like I was getting secret files from the FBI, but seeing her reaction I wasted no time going to medical records and having them print out a hard copy. There it was, in black and white, Katherine had the rash, the rash that was a perfect circle. The pieces of the puzzle were coming together.

+ + +

The woman from the support group had suggested I watch the documentary *Under Our Skin*. She told me IGeneX was the gold standard of Lyme disease testing and explained some of the complexities around diagnostics and testing. It was a lot to take in.

As I watched the documentary, tears streamed down my face. I saw my daughter reflected on the screen in the character's stories. Over and over again, people just like Katherine sought medical care as they grew progressively sicker. Symptoms were often dismissed and misdiagnosed, until they went out of pocket, to these Lyme-literate doctors, where they finally got the care they needed, and then there were stories of recovery and hope. But it all came at a cost. Insurance companies routinely denied coverage for treatment, quoting government guidelines. These guidelines called for narrowly defined protocols, protocols that were leaving many patients sick and the Lyme community in an uproar.

I started to understand the reaction I got from the doctor who dropped us so abruptly from her panel. This was no ordinary disease. Astonishingly, it was a *controversial disease*, a *political disease*, just like the Tick Talk lady had said. It was all starting to sink in, and it felt like a betrayal.

I had put so much trust and faith in the medical system we were in, to think that it would fail us for so long--that it could fail a *sick child*. I did not fully understand all the controversy and confusion around Lyme disease, but Katherine was my sick child, and I was going to do everything in my power to see that she had the treatment she needed to get well.

I filed a grievance at Kaiser. It was the process required to request an outside referral. I wanted her to see a Lyme specialist, one of these Lyme-literate doctors I was now hearing so much about. The request was denied. Kaiser assigned us yet another doctor, a pediatrician they called a "puzzler."

+ + +

Marge arrived at the hospital with the sandwiches, her kids in tow. My dear friend was standing there in that awful place, the PICU, where Katherine lay. My worlds collided. She was my good friend from Bible study, my friend whom I had lunch with every week. We shared prayer requests and talked about our kids and their schools. She handed me the bag. Her little girl looked pale, "I don't feel well." It was a wretched place.

Marge gave me a hug, "It will sink in later," she said.

+ + +

It became clear Kaiser was not going to do anything about Lyme disease. Our new doctor, "the puzzler," denied the cardiologist ever suggested dysautonomia, "It's just deconditioning," he said. I started to feel like Alice in Wonderland, *"through the looking glass."* I needed perspective and answers, so I turned to my doctor. I trusted her. She was outside of Kaiser and had nothing to gain or lose by advising me about Lyme disease. She had always been reasonable with me. She explained how deeply divided the medical community truly was and suggested we get a second opinion at a local clinic that specializes in treating Lyme patients.

It seemed every aspect of Lyme had conflicting information, and testing was on top of the controversy. Kaiser gave Katherine the ELISA test (pronounced exactly like my first name), which came back negative. This was not surprising because it is known for its high rate of false negatives, especially in advanced stages. My doctor said she did not like to use the ELISA, "It's not sensitive enough," she said, and explained that while there was no perfect Lyme test, she preferred the Western Blot. "If one or two bands are positive with symptoms, I consider a clinical diagnosis." Over three bands with symptoms was more clearly Lyme disease. She ordered a test for me and none of the bands came back positive. Later Katherine would have this test done and over five bands would test positive, but Kaiser would not accept her test results because they came from an outside lab, and yet they refused to administer the same test themselves. We had fallen into the rabbit hole of Lyme disease.

+ + +

I called the local Lyme clinic. We needed a second opinion. I prayed for God's guidance. "God is the God of truth," I thought, and prayed for Him to reveal the truth about Lyme disease to me.

The week before our first appointment I decided to drive by the clinic. It was just an ordinary looking office building on the industrial side of Santa Rosa, near the airport. I paced around the parking lot, peeking in windows trying to get a feel for the place. I had made a vow we would not go down any medical roads that conflicted with Biblical values. A lot of alternative medicine seemed to include spirituality, but not spirituality I was comfortable with. "God honors those who honor Him," I always told Katherine. There would be no blessing in seeking treatment that conflicted with our Christian values. I begged God to show me if we were going in the right direction and prayed for a sign.

When I got back to the car I had a message from Marge on my phone. She had been at church that morning and a woman from Bible study showed up who she had not seen in months. She had been in treatment for Lyme disease. Marge told her about Katherine and her friend recommended we go to this very clinic. As I was standing in front of the clinic praying for a sign, asking God to show me if this was the right direction, Marge was leaving me a message telling me about her friend.

THREE

Dr. A greeted us, a pretty young blonde with a twinkle in her eyes. She told us she used to work at Kaiser but wanted to spend more time with her patients. I was relieved by how mainstream she seemed, a conventional doctor. She told us her story. She was sick as a young child and, like Katherine, her mother took her to doctor after doctor, never able to find answers. This was what inspired her to go into medicine. She wanted to help people and it showed. There was something about her that was different than the other doctors we had seen. For the first time in years, in a doctor's office, I started to let my guard down.

I had gotten so used to advocating, for fighting for doctors to take Katherine's symptoms seriously. Every lab test, every specialist appointment, every step of the way with Kaiser had felt like pushing a boulder uphill only to have it roll back over us, and suddenly I could let go and this doctor was actually taking the reins. I was secondary to the appointment. Her sole focus was on Katherine.

She spoke directly to Katherine and then listened, actually listened, to her answers. It seemed so obvious, but nobody had asked Katherine about her pain before. Dr. A asked her how severe it was, on a scale from one to ten, how often she was in pain and for how long.

I found out for the first time that my sweet Katherine had been living in a chronic pain scale of six or higher, every minute of every day for years. She could not remember the last time she was not in pain. The days I picked her up from school were seven to eight days. Good days for her were a five or six. I felt sick to my stomach. I felt furious. My eyes welled up with tears. In all the years we had taken Katherine to doctor after doctor, not one of them had ever asked her how much pain she was in or how often. Instead they just kept insisting she needed a therapist.

I reported back to The Puzzler what Dr. A had said, but he just gave us stern warnings against "Lyme charlatans." Yet he provided no alternative. It seemed more than a division, the two sides actually contradicted one another. As a mother I found myself in the position of having to navigate a crossroads with my daughter's health at the center. No matter which road we went down, we had doctors on the other side telling us it was the wrong direction. Kaiser doctors insisted it was all a matter of the mind, and offered no treatment, but warned against the Lyme doctors. The Lyme doctors offered treatment, and warned that the illness would continue to progress without intervention. This divide was in every aspect of Lyme disease from testing to treating, and it was not unique to Kaiser. The entire medical community was polarized about Lyme disease. There seemed to be no middle ground. I had to decide between trusting Kaiser doctors or the Lyme clinic.

I was not a doctor. I was a mother with a very sick child. I needed wisdom. I needed truth. I needed this division in the medical community to end and for my daughter to get the health care she so desperately needed. I kept praying for God to show me the right direction.

+ + +

I was exhausted from researching Lyme disease and

had made dinner plans with friends. Feeling like terrible company, I wanted to cancel, but we were celebrating our friend Carly's birthday, and it had been a difficult evening to plan. Times and dates and locations kept changing, until we finally settled on a Friday evening at a restaurant in downtown Santa Rosa.

As I pulled into town, instead of going to the residential streets where I usually parked for free, I found myself driving into a metered lot. In all the years I had driven to Santa Rosa, I had never once paid for parking. It was as though I was on autopilot and even as I was pulling into the lot, parking and paying the meter, I kept wondering, *"Why am I doing this?"* but something compelled me forward.

My friends wanted to know how Katherine was doing and I told them about our appointment earlier that week at the Lyme clinic with Dr. A. "I know her," Carly said, "She goes to my church. She's there tonight."

I had unknowingly parked in the lot right next to their church and walked by as Dr. A was inside helping her husband set up a concert he had organized for that very night. All the time and date changes of this dinner had led us exactly to the same moment Dr. A would be at church just a few blocks away.

When dinner was over Carly insisted on walking me to my car and stopping by to say hello. As we stood in their crowded church, Dr. A and I laughed; neither of us were surprised the other was a Christian. "You can see it in the eyes," she said. I had the exact same thought. And then she looked at me in all seriousness and said, "I am going to help your daughter."

+ + +

21

The Lyme test came back positive, "CDC positive," Dr. A said.

"What does that mean?" I asked. It meant Katherine's results were reportable to the Center for Disease Control and Prevention. She had over five bands positive with textbook symptoms, a clear-cut case of Lyme disease. "Great news," I thought, "now I can go back to Kaiser and they will cover her treatment."

The Puzzler refused to accept Katherine's test results, saying that the lab was not certified and as evidence he sent me a link to a newspaper article profiling a patient who had a false positive test from this lab. The article was over ten years old. I asked him for something more current but he dismissed my concerns insisting the lab was not certified. Wanting to know the truth, I called IgeneX. They assured me they were fully certified and directed me to their website where they had copies of their certification online. According to the Lyme doctors they were the gold standard testing for Lyme disease, but it did not matter. The Puzzler would not accept Dr. A's diagnosis or Katherine's lab results. At the same time, he would not give Katherine a Kaiser issued Western Blot test, insisting only on using the ELISA test, which was widely documented as unreliable for diagnostics.

He referred us to the Infectious Disease Department and I made an appointment. "Where has Katherine traveled?" the specialist wanted to know.

"She's been to the east coast, as a little girl," my mind flashed back to her running through fields of grass in Vermont with her cousins, "and to Florida." My father lived in the swamps of northern Florida and we had visited him there. The kids called him Grandpa Chicken because he kept a flock of chickens, each one individually named. He mimicked animal noises for their entertainment as they searched for eggs on his farm.

She wanted to know where else Katherine had been

that could have exposed her to ticks. Every summer we spent weekends in the redwoods, and there was the time we had been hiking on the coast near Mendocino and came back to the car covered in ticks. I told her about the nature trail behind Katherine's school, the oak tree in our back yard she loved to climb, and our dogs who Katherine snuck into her bed to read stories to.

I told her about the rash when she was seven, and how that marked the beginning of her symptoms, symptoms that grew progressively worse every year until she could hardly make it through a school day. I told her about how Katherine had been an active child who could not even ride her bike anymore because of the pain. We went through an exhaustive history and at the end of it she emphatically said, "It is not Lyme disease." There was no equivocation.

"But the rash, the exposure, the symptoms, the CDC positive test result?" I asked.

"It is absolutely not Lyme disease," she insisted.

I could accept doubt. I could accept reservation, but I was not prepared for absolutes. "If it's not Lyme disease, then what else could it be?" I asked, "What other direction can we go in?"

She had made up her mind, "There is no other direction to go in. It's not Lyme disease. The mind does amazing things."

There was nothing left to say. "...the mind does amazing things." The appointment was over. "Absolutely not Lyme...the mind does amazing things." We had talked for over an hour. I was reeling, her words playing back in my head like a broken record.

"The mind does amazing things." That was her only answer. For the first time in my daughter's sickness, I sat down and sobbed.

Our world was spinning upside down, and this

strange world of Lyme disease did not seem to rely on facts or even rational thinking. It was *The Emperor has no Clothes*, only reversed. I felt like I was looking at a tree and the doctor was telling me it was not there, but I could see it; the wind rustling through the leaves, a bird landing. I trusted my own senses enough to see that Lyme disease was real. My daughter had the exposure, the rash, the symptoms, and the positive test result. "The mind does amazing things." "Yes," I thought, "the mind really does do amazing things." We had reached the end of the road at Kaiser. If there was a question about what direction to take, it was over. My daughter was sick. She needed treatment. We were going to have to pay out of pocket and go to the Lyme clinic. I prayed for God to provide.

FOUR

Dr. A told us she was moving across the country. Her husband got a great job in Texas. I was devastated. We had been through so many doctors and finally found one who we liked and trusted. She assured me her colleagues at the clinic would do a great job. Katherine and I met her for coffee and she gave me her personal phone number and told us to call or text her any time. We had formed a bond in our short time together. While she could not treat Katherine moving forward, she was invested in her, and offered to be a sounding board for us if we had any questions.

We met Dr. L, Katherine's new doctor at the clinic, and reviewed her medical history. Dr. A had started her on oral antibiotics. We were told IV antibiotics were the best option, but we could not afford them. It was a horrible feeling making medical decisions for one's child based on cost, but we had to work within our means. Katherine had been sick for a long time. Treatment was going to take a while and it was expensive. Dr. L worked out a protocol combining antibiotics with herbal remedies and immediately we saw results. By the end of summer, Katherine was having symptom free days for the first time in years. By early fall, she had started her freshman year of high school, was earning straight-A's and had joined the debate team. Things were looking good and we finally had hope.

The Puzzler had agreed to monitor Katherine's liver labs while she was in treatment, as liver damage can be a potential side effect of long term antibiotics. He emailed me alarmed that her labs were testing high, and strongly recommended we stop the antibiotics. Dr. L thought a break might be a good idea and said we could use an herbal protocol while giving her liver a rest.

Two weeks later I got the dreaded phone call. It was a Tuesday morning in early October and I was just getting out of Bible study. It was Katherine, "I feel sick Mom, please come get me." She went home, crawled into bed and did not get out again for the better part of nine months.

FIVE

I wanted to sleep. I was so tired. I put a pillow over my head trying to block out the sound. The girl next to us was so close. All that separated us was a thin curtain. "Don't cry," the nurse said. And then I realized God put me on the other side of this curtain. It was our first day in the PICU, but I had a job to do. I could be a prayer warrior for the families around us. "Don't cry," she said again, and I began to pray.

Something was happening on the 10th floor, something bigger than Katherine and I, something strange and mysterious. I could not help but wonder why we were in the PICU at the same time as Beth, Matt and Lilly. Katherine and Lilly had been treated in the same bed at the emergency room in Santa Rosa, our pastor had commented on it. In all the years he had been in ministry, he had never had two kids in his congregation in the PICU at the same time. I wondered too, why were both our families up there?

I thought back to Bible study. I remembered an elderly woman recalling a hospital stay. She was placed in a room with a loud, complaining roommate who kept her up at night and gave her no peace during the day. She wanted to ask to change rooms, but then she realized, God brought her there for a reason. She decided instead of focusing on her own comfort, to pray for God to show her how to bless her roommate. She noticed her roommate was alone and that nobody came to visit her, so she reached out, and they became friends. Her roommate passed away with a loving, kind, Christian friend at her side.

As she told this story, she pointed out how much she wanted to request a new room, but in the end she made a friend and her roommate did not die alone. I thought of that story and my surroundings on the 10th floor. If Katherine had to be up there, then I was going to pray for opportunities for God to use me to bless others. There had to be a greater purpose in all this.

+ + +

A Home and Hospital teacher was assigned to come to our house once a week with schoolwork. We tried putting Katherine back on antibiotics, but nothing worked. Days turned into weeks turned into months of her bedridden and in constant pain. We tried every kind of diet recommended for Lyme disease: gluten free, soy, dairy and corn free, no nightshades, no sugar, nothing refined. Soon the list of what she could eat was shorter then what she could not. I made pots of bone broth to boost her immune system and we followed a complex herbal protocol along with every combination of oral antibiotics imaginable. Day in, day out, she lay in a darkened room, her headaches so severe the light hurt her eyes. She was lost in the darkness of this disease, into what I called the "Lyme coma." There was a veil of pain between my daughter and the world. She could not even join me to watch television or share a meal. I felt like I had lost my daughter.

I called Dr. A. She could not give me outright medical advice, but she offered suggestions to bring up with Dr. L, and once again IV antibiotics came up. "They bypass the gut and go right into the blood stream." They were just so expensive, but at this point, we had no other choice. Katherine was not getting better. Every step of the way God had provided, a grant here, a check from a friend or family member there. Just when we needed the next phase of her treatment, something would come through. Always on the edge, we were never destitute. God had faithfully provided, and so I knew that if this was the right direction, He would provide for this too.

Dr. A knew a doctor at Kaiser who "believes in Lyme." Her panel was full, but on Dr. A's recommendation she accepted Katherine. I was glad to be rid of The Puzzler. Katherine had been bedridden for months under his care. It was his advice to stop the antibiotics, and then he offered no solutions to help her get better.

A local Lyme support group had organized a meeting with the head of Sonoma County Department of Health and I wanted to attend. Patients poured into a room in a church basement. As they told their stories I noticed reoccurring themes. Over and over again, stories of denial of coverage, people who lost houses to pay for medical care, former athletes now disabled, people with masters degrees unable to read a paragraph. It was terrifying to listen to how ravaged these people had become by this disease, and every one of them had been misdiagnosed for years and refused care by their insurance companies.

There was anger in the room. Anger at the medical system that denied their disease, denied their treatment. Over and over again one name came up, Dr. Black. Apparently he was the chief of Kaiser's area Infectious Disease Department and apparently he "did not believe in Lyme disease." Patients talked about how they were labeled as "Lyme Loonies" and once they mentioned they had Lyme disease they were denied care for any other residual health issues.

"There is no Lyme disease in California," we had been told, or that it was so rare we should not be concerned, but just the other day, I read in the newspaper that Stanford had done a study testing ticks in Bay Area parks. One of the most popular parks in Santa Rosa had the highest rate of Lyme disease. There was Lyme disease in California. That had been proven, and yet the medical world seemed to be in deep denial, beyond logic, beyond reason, beyond facts. There was a calculated denial of care and that denial, as I sat at this round table, listening to the stories of the people affected by this disease, was destroying lives.

+ + +

We met with Dr. F, Katherine's new doctor at Kaiser. She offered to call Dr. Black personally, "but it won't do any good. He doesn't believe in Lyme disease." There it was again. How could a doctor, a head of a department, not believe in a well-documented disease? That is like saying, "I don't believe in gravity." Maybe, but it still exists. Dr. F went on to suggest that Katherine see a therapist, "just to rule things out," not because Katherine needed one, she insisted, but because she thought it would help to convince Infectious Disease of her Lyme diagnosis.

I was not so sure. If a bulls-eye rash, exposure, symptoms, a positive test result, response to treatment, and then this reaction to stopping treatment did not convince them, I had a hard time believing one visit to a therapist would change their minds. At this point I was suspicious of this push toward psychology. It was relentless. And it was an ambiguous road.

Katherine had the *"peace that passes understanding"* (Philippians 4:4-7). Despite living in a chronic pain scale of six to eight, despite losing all her friends, activities, high school and being confined to bed, she truly had peace. How could I explain that she had the best counselor of all, Jesus, and that He ministered to her heart and mind, day in and day out?

She told me, "All those years of church and Sunday school, things pastors and Christians have said to me are in my heart and come to mind when I am in pain." She was able to tolerate the pain because God Himself was ministering to her. Welling up from her heart were Bible verses, sermons and testimonies that comforted her. Anyone who spent time with Katherine remarked on the peace they felt in her presence. It was truly supernatural, and it was a peace none of her doctors would accept. Seeing a therapist would not make a difference. What Katherine needed was a Kaiser doctor to take her seriously and provide the medical care she so desperately needed.

+ + +

Christmas was around the corner and Katherine had been bedridden for months. Every Sunday I was hopeful she would be well enough to go to church for prayer by our pastor at the cross, but every Sunday she remained bedridden, until finally I asked him to come over to our house and pray.

"Is anyone among you sick? Let them call the elders of the church to pray over them and anoint them with oil in the name of the Lord." (James 5:14)

I was anxious for our pastor and the elders to arrive. They were on their way to our house to pray for Katherine. I believed in the power of prayer. I had seen it work over and over again. This was important medicine. Pacing around waiting for them, I knew I needed to get quiet before God, and so I turned on a Christian music station and sat at my kitchen table. I felt so lost in the darkness of Lyme disease, in the loss of my daughter. I needed assurance of God's presence and

31

peace.

"Holy, Holy, Holy! Lord God Almighty" began to play and just as it did a ray of sunshine beamed through my kitchen window and landed on me like a spotlight. I sat there bathed in sunlight listening and praying through the hymn. *"...Holy, holy, holy! Merciful and mighty, God in three persons, blessed Trinity."* The song was over. Just as it ended clouds covered the sunbeam. I sat up and there was a knock on the door.

My pastor had arrived with two men from church. I led them to Katherine's room. He pulled out a pretty little blue bottle filled with anointing oil and I slipped out of the room. They stood over Katherine's bed as they lay hands on her and prayed.

"I felt the Holy Spirit in there," my pastor said when they came out. This gave me peace.

SIX

It was time for Katherine to try IV antibiotics. Dr. L wanted her to start with a Hep-Lock, which they would insert at the clinic, and then she would go home and I would train in administering her medicine through it. This was the best option, it was explained to us, to see how she tolerated the antibiotics through her bloodstream. She would have the IV in four days on and three days off.

For the first time in her treatment I felt a sense of dread. I could not explain it, but something about the IV was unsettling and I could not shake it. The day before our appointment our pipes froze and burst. We had no running water. A dark cloud covered me as I went to Bible study that morning. I needed prayers from these faithful women of God.

After Bible study, Mary approached me. Her husband was a contractor and he would come and fix our pipes later that day for free. She would not hear of accepting anything for it, "Don't you dare interfere with our blessing," she joked.

And there it was, that cold cup of water given to us in our need. God was teaching me deeply in this: "...*if anyone gives even a cup of cold water to one of these little ones who is my disciple, truly I tell you, that person will certainly not lose their reward*" (Matthew 10:42).

Mary called to check in that evening. Her husband and son had already come out to the house and fixed the pipe. We had running water.

"This is going to sound like a strange question," she said, "but do you want a Christmas tree?"

Christmas was less then two weeks away but I could not bring myself to get a tree without Katherine. Like most families, we had our traditions, and the thought of picking one out without her proved impossible. I could not do it, and yet I could not imagine Christmas without a tree. This became a secret prayer of my heart.

Just days before Mary's call, a couple came by to visit from church and asked if we needed anything. I desperately wanted to ask them to go pick out a Christmas tree for us, but I could not get the words out. After they left, I resigned myself to a treeless Christmas. I was even beginning to wonder if we should celebrate at all.

"Do you want a Christmas tree? I buy one from our church every year and give it away and this year you came to mind," Mary was worried she might offend me. Little did she know how much this meant to me, that I had been praying that someone would think of us, because I was just not able to get the words out to ask.

"You have no idea how much," I responded, tears glistening in my eyes. We would have Christmas after all.

Before nightfall, her son had dropped a Christmas tree on our porch. It reminded me of the one in the *Nutcracker* that magically grew bigger. Ours had that same quality as it filled up our living room in the most magnificent way. It was the most beautiful Christmas tree I had ever seen. I bought clear glass ornaments that reflected the lights and tinsel, and decorated it with all our favorite ornaments from past Christmases. I called it our Holy Spirit tree. It was our Christmas miracle and a reminder of answered prayers, even the secret ones in our heart God hears.

+ + +

A friend met us at the Lyme clinic for Katherine's first IV treatment. Her daughter had gone through a similar treatment. "You look pale," she said to me as we were escorted to a back room where patients in plush chairs sat engrossed in laptops or quietly talking. IV poles stood next to them with tubes dripping medicine into their arms. A nurse pulled Katherine's shirtsleeve up in search of a vein. She tapped and poked several times and then left in search of another nurse. They pricked her tender arm over and over again concluding, "She doesn't have good veins." Her veins were apparently too deep for a Hep-Lock. They could not do the treatment. A huge wave of relief washed over me. I had prayed before we went in, and so I felt confident if this was not possible, it was not God's will, and she would find treatment another way.

"You're color is back," my friend joked in the parking lot. Katherine was calm every step of the way, trusting in God completely, modeling a mature Christian spirit well beyond her years.

+ + +

"Pilgrim was taken to a large upper room that faced the sunrise. And the name of that room was Peace."
-The Pilgrim's Progress

"I don't mind being sick," Katherine said to me, more concerned over my sadness than her own suffering.

"What do you mean you don't mind?" I asked.

"When I was a little girl in Sunday School," she confessed, "I told God He could use my life. God allowed this. He has a purpose," she said with total certainty. Katherine had given her life to God to use according to His will when she was a small child and had pondered this all these years, but never said anything. She only told me in order to comfort me, and for me to understand that she had peace about her illness. She truly believed that this was all part of God's plan and that He was in control.

Katherine was at peace, trusting God. I was fighting for her with everything I had. Fighting with prayer, advocating with the doctors. We were in the Lyme wars and I was on the battlefield for my daughter. But she had peace. She did not need to fight because she knew that God in heaven, Jesus Himself was interceding on her behalf and she trusted Him and accepted His will completely, even if that meant laying in bed in terrible pain, missing out on her freshman year of high school, having her friends forget her, making her life fit into the length of her bed. "If just one person gets saved as a result of my sickness, it is worth it," she said. She meant it.

+ + +

The nurse held up a needle. It was huge. More like a shot for a horse than a young girl. Her doctor wanted to try antibiotic shots since the Hep-Lock did not work and I was supposed to be training to administer them at home. The only problem was my squeamishness. Katherine requested me at blood draws, not for the maternal support, but because she found it funny that I would get so woozy and nearly pass out at the sight of blood, while she sat there calmly, vial after vial getting filled.

The nurse was talking, explaining what I would need to do, but I was not hearing a word she was saying, eyes fixed on the impossibly large needle. I felt my mind go fuzzy. The room was spinning and at the center was this giant needle. The nurse got up and left the room. I turned to Katherine, "Where is she going?"

"She said she has to check with Dr. L about the dose," Katherine had followed every word.

She was gone a long time and I started to pray. I could not imagine injecting Katherine with this needle. When she finally returned, my prayers were answered. The nurse explained I would not be able to give the shots at home. They were giving us donated medicine, which saved us hundreds of dollars, but the policy was that it had to be administered at the clinic. For fifteen dollars a visit, a certified nurse would give the shot. "Thank you Jesus," I thought as she escorted Katherine behind a curtain. The nurse filled the torturous needle with medicine and slowly injected it into Katherine.

SEVEN

A mother carries her child's sickness everywhere she goes. I began to meet other moms with sick children and we formed a prayer group, meeting every Thursday morning to pray for our kids. I served in Bible study as a discussion group leader and every week put a prayer request in with the other leaders to pray for my daughter. I was greedy for prayer and had no pride in asking for it. Every prayer warrior I knew I put on the job of praying for Katherine.

The New Year came and Katherine remained bedridden. Her school contacted us and told us they would no longer provide Home and Hospital. A meeting was arranged with her vice principal and guidance counselor. They informed me they could not accommodate Katherine bedridden and suggested we would be better off elsewhere. We were always welcome back, when Katherine was healthy. The only accommodation they were willing to make was to place her in the "special needs" classroom where she could get "individualized attention," which was a moot point because Katherine was physically unable to go to school. She was also a straight-A student and I did not want her education compromised because she was sick. Surely they had encountered sick children before? But they insisted their school was not equipped to meet her needs. They smiled as they showed me the door.

Katherine was bedridden and we no longer had a high school for her to attend. They had given me a phone number for a nearby school that specialized in independent study, suggesting that would be a better fit, but when I called, they told me they were full. I went to the local office of education on a tip that they would provide curriculum for home study. The man I met with spent the entire meeting complaining about his supervisor, who apparently had missed the deadline for accreditation, and so none of their course work would qualify for college admission. He explained to me that the work she had done at her high school was non-transferable. She would have to start all over, from the beginning, for each class. We were in no-man's-land educationally and it was a mess.

I went to school after school seeking accommodation and was turned away for this reason or that. Every meeting left me more discouraged than the one before. Never in my wildest dreams did I imagine having a sick child meant no options for education, and yet that was where we were. I did not want to home school. I already had so much on my plate, and yet it was beginning to look like that was our only option. We were running out of resources, paying out of pocket for medical care and now we would have to find the resources to pay for her school curriculum too.

+ + +

April was standing by the cross as I walked by after church one Sunday, and she asked if I wanted to pray. She knew Katherine's story and said that she had a friend who home schooled her children and might be a good resource.

Jane came over with a stack of books and taught me the process of starting an independent school, including filling out an affidavit with the state. She was home schooling one of her daughters but the rest of her four kids went to the independent school we had been recommended to try, but was full. She suggested I call back and try to enroll her for the following year. That made sense. It seemed like a good program and the best of both worlds. The school provided a teacher and curriculum, which the students worked on independently at home. It sounded a lot like Home and Hospital and certainly better than my trying to navigate a college-bound high school education. I was not giving up on Katherine's dreams for her future just because she was sick.

I set up a meeting at the school and an older woman met with me and escorted me to a classroom divided by cubicles that served as offices. Some kids sat at a desk nearby working on homework. Jane had spoken highly of the program, but I needed more information about how they could accommodate Katherine. The woman I met with was not interested in talking about the school. She wanted to know what was going on with Katherine's health. I gave her an overview, but she pressed for details and kept asking questions. It started to feel like an assault. I tried to get the conversation back to the school, but she kept on swinging with questions. It was getting personal. *Left hook, right hook, bam, bam, bam*, she would not let up. My face turned red, voice shaking, "Please stop," I said. But the questions kept coming. She was taking pleasure in this. Her eyes flickered.

"Please, stop," I said again, louder this time, "I just want to know if you can help my daughter. She needs a school."

Her eyes flickered again, *"You know your daughter's a truant, don't you?"* Knock out punch.

I was mentally staggering. She watched with a smile on her face. I stood up, "My daughter is sick. We need a school. Either you can help us or not." I found my way out to my car, too upset to drive home. I sat in the driver's seat trying to collect myself.

I looked up and walking across the campus was

Jane. "My son forgot a book," she said, "I'm not usually here at this time."

That Sunday I went to church and my pastor preached about Paul's nephew overhearing a plot to kill him and how God used that to save Paul's life. While I was in church listening to that sermon, Jane was attending service at a different church in Sebastopol. Sitting next to her was a teacher named Susan. It turned out Susan had been on the other side of the partition during that awful meeting at the school and had overheard the entire conversation.

Susan offered to meet me for coffee. She told me she would advocate for Katherine and offered to take her on as her personal student. She was true to her word and Katherine was enrolled in the school for the following year, with a Christian teacher. She would be Katherine's head teacher for the remainder of high school. God is good.

+ + +

As I lay in the PICU next to Katherine, listening to the nurse on the other side of the curtain say, "don't cry," I knew that God had placed me there, just as He had placed Susan. I was the Christian on the other side of the curtain now and I had a job to do. I began to pray. I prayed for God to calm the spirit of that poor girl and to guide the doctors and nurses in her care. I heard the sound of a drill, and I kept praying and did not stop praying until it was all over. Later that week, I saw her walking the halls with her dad, doing the hospital loop, and I thanked Jesus.

EIGHT

The shots were too painful to continue long term. Katherine never complained but confided that the pain kept her up for days afterward. She tolerated the antibiotics through her bloodstream and so Dr. L determined it was time to try a PICC line, a surgically implanted IV. She told us about a clinic in Sacramento that specialized in PICC lines and only charged a fraction of what it would cost to have it done in Santa Rosa. It was a two-hour drive to the state's capital, but it seemed like the best option. We had hope for her healing, and if it meant driving to a clinic in Sacramento, that was where we were going.

Dr. F said that she could arrange for nursing care through Kaiser's home nurse program. I had resigned myself that the bulk of Katherine's medical care would be out of pocket. I just wanted her to get the treatment she needed. It felt terribly unjust for her to be fully insured and yet not have coverage, but I had nothing left in me to fight it. My fight was for Katherine's health. At this point, I was grateful for any help we could get from Kaiser.

Katherine needed a nurse to change her dressing and check her PICC line twenty-four hours after insertion. After that, she would require regular injections, flushing, and sterile dressing changes. The Lyme clinic offered trainings to do it all at home, but they were expensive, and nursing was an area that made me very uncomfortable, especially with my daughter as the patient. Much to my relief, the referral at Kaiser was approved. I got a call from the home nursing department and everything was set up. Her PICC line was scheduled late on a Friday afternoon and the nurse would come to our house on Saturday.

+ + +

We drove to Sacramento and were the last patients of the day as we watched the clinic's busy waiting room empty out. When Katherine's name was finally called, a nurse named Bill escorted us into a back room where Katherine was outfitted in hospital scrubs while I signed consent forms. Everything happened so quickly. The next thing I knew she had the PICC line in her arm and we were saying goodbye, thanking the medical staff. While we were still in the clinic lobby my phone rang. I recognized the number. It was from Kaiser. They were canceling her home nursing care.

"It is not Kaiser policy to provide nursing care for a procedure done outside of Kaiser," the nurse said.

"But she just had the PICC line inserted," I protested. "It's already in her arm. It is 5 p.m. on a Friday night. What are we supposed to do?" I begged, I pleaded, but she would not budge. "Kaiser knew it was an outside clinic when we set it up. Her doctor knew. The nurse who set up the home visit knew. Everyone knew."

Her dressing had to be changed within twenty-four hours. The clinic was closing behind us as we made our way to the car. Friday evening lights were twinkling as day turned into evening.

"It is not Kaiser policy," she repeated, standing her ground.

"Is it Kaiser policy to hurt children?!" I bellowed

back, hanging up the phone. There was nothing more to say. Her nursing care had been cancelled.

I sat in the car, head in my hands, tears streaming down my face. Katherine was in the backseat, PICC line freshly implanted in her arm. My phone buzzed. It was Dr. A. She was checking in to see how things were going.

I told her what happened and she started calling all her nursing friends in the Bay Area to see if any one could make a home visit, but none of them were available. Dr. A was in Texas. She had done her best to help us. She told me what to look for in case of infection. The Lyme clinic would be open on Monday. We would be able to go in then for a nurse to change her dressing and I would start the trainings. As we drove home, I thought of the Tick Talk lady, and how when I first talked to her she seemed so conspiratorial to me, but now I understood. This disease could make you crazy, the injustice of a disease where denied care is standard protocol. Lyme disease was being compared to AIDS in the 1980's. It was a matter of time, everyone said, but we did not have time. My child was sick now.

+ + +

Kaiser had just finished building a brand new state of the art hospital and had already started moving patients in. We could see it from the 10th floor window and we kept hearing how wonderful it would be. "You can order food directly from the TV, just like room service," a nurse boasted. Game consoles for every child and parents would be provided a real bed, shower, microwave, refrigerator and coffee maker in every room along with a workstation. Every nurse and doctor who came by could barely contain their enthusiasm, beginning and ending every visit with "when we are in the new hospital..." They were getting ready to move, as the hospital emptied out floor by floor beneath us. Pediatrics would be the last to go. But we were not in the new hospital, and hopefully would never be.

As I looked out at the shiny new building across the street, I thought, "What a perfect metaphor for Lyme disease." I could see the future of care. I could cross the street and walk inside the lobby of the new hospital, but it was not our reality. Our reality was the old hospital. Our reality was a deeply divided medical community who could not agree on one aspect of Lyme disease from testing to treatment, and this divide was fuel for insurance companies to deny treatment to patients in need.

We were standing in a point of Lyme history where there was a ground swelling taking place. From where we stood, I could practically see the future of Lyme disease. Research is being done on better diagnostics and doctors are fine-tuning protocols. More and more celebrities are coming out with Lyme disease, drawing attention to it, and laws are starting to change, forcing better treatment options. It seems like everyone knows someone with Lyme disease. The status quo could not continue, and yet no matter how bright the future was for Lyme patients, Katherine was sick now.

NINE

A tall man with dark hair walked in pushing an IV pole, "Hi, I'm Jacob." We were at Kaiser because Dr. F wanted to take a look at Katherine's PICC line. She was trying to placate me over my outrage about the canceled nursing care and had agreed to an office visit. She brought in Jacob to do a saline flush and check her insertion sight. Dr. F left us in his care. Once she was out of the room, he turned to me and asked about a book I was holding. It was about Lyme disease. "My wife has that," he said. As he tended to Katherine's PICC line he asked more questions and before our appointment was over he offered to help. He would personally change Katherine's PICC line dressing every week.

I had already trained at the Lyme clinic in sterile dressing changes and administering her medicine at home, but I did not feel confident with it. Jacob was a gift from God. We would have a trained nurse to care for her, as it should be. Nurse Jacob was yet another answer to prayer.

+ + +

There is a story in the Bible where a man brings his son to Jesus to be healed. He had already asked the disciples, but they were unable to heal the boy. Jesus rebukes them all for their lack of faith. The father says to

47

Jesus, *"If you can, please take pity on us and heal him."*

Jesus responds, *"If you can?' Everything is possible for one who believes."*

Immediately the man exclaimed, *"I do believe; help me with my unbelief!"* Jesus then healed the boy (Mark 17:17-27).

"I believe Jesus; help me with my unbelief," became my prayer. I had faith, but it was messy and mixed with the fear my daughter would never get out of bed. My church was praying. The moms in my prayer group were praying. Friends and family were praying. The ladies from Bible study were praying. The most godly, devoted Christians I knew were praying, and yet she was not getting better.

"One day Katherine will get up and walk," my pastor said as I was leaving church one Sunday. He had gone through a bone marrow transplant. He was no stranger to sickness. He was a godly man who preached the Bible chapter by chapter, verse by verse every week. I trusted his spiritual wisdom completely, and yet I doubted his word. Nothing was making her better. The doctors were starting to question her treatment. It was not working. I was losing hope.

"I believe Lord Jesus; help me with my unbelief," became the only prayer I had left in me.

+ + +

"'Imitate those who faith and patience inherit what has been promised' (Hebrews 6:12).

The biblical heroes of faith call us from the heights they have won, encouraging us that what man once did, man can do again. They remind us not only of the necessity of faith but also of the patience required for faith's work to be perfected. May we fear attempting to remove ourselves too soon from the hands of our heavenly Guide, or missing even one lesson of His loving discipline due to our discouragement or doubt.

An old village blacksmith once said, 'There is only one thing I fear: being thrown onto the scrap heap. You see, in order to strengthen a piece of steel, I must first temper it. I heat it, hammer it, and then quickly plunge it into a bucket of cold water. Very soon I know whether it will fall to pieces. If, after one or two tests, I see it will not allow itself to be tempered, I throw it onto the scrap heap, only to later sell it to the junkman for a few cents a pound.

'I realize the Lord tests me in the same way: through fire, water and heavy blows of His hammer. If I am unwilling to withstand the test, or prove unfit for His tempering process, I am afraid he may throw me in the scrap heap.'

When the fire in your life is the hottest stand still, for '*later on...it produces a harvest*' (Heb. 12:11) of blessings. Then we will be able to say with Job, '*When he has tested me, I will come forth as gold*' (Job 23:10)."

-Streams in the Dessert

I felt that pressure. I felt God's fire, water and heavy blows. I could barely take any of it any longer. I did not think I could withstand any more without breaking. Bible study ended for summer break and Katherine continued to be bedridden and sick. I started to lose hope of her ever getting better. I resigned myself to a life with a permanently bedridden child, living out her life in a darkened room. Any hopes I had for her future were dimming in light of her constant pain. We had reached the end of the road and had nowhere left to go. I was preparing myself for a life that began and ended at the foot of her bed.

TEN

Jacob called me into his office. He wanted to talk to me privately, away from Katherine. Someone in Kaiser management found out he had been changing her PICC line dressing and he was told he had to stop providing nursing care for her. I knew he had a wife and baby at home. He would be putting his job in jeopardy if he continued. I was grateful for the help he had provided. He sent us home with a bag of supplies and wished us well.

Katherine's Lyme doctor wanted to give her system a rest from medicine and take her off the antibiotics for a few weeks. I was nervous after what happened the last time. Pulling the plug on antibiotics was what landed us in this mess of her being bedridden in the first place, but at the same time, nothing seemed to be working. Maybe a break would be good for her. Maybe the medication was part of the problem.

Just a few days after stopping antibiotics, her symptoms increased dramatically. She started getting chills, shaking all over, teeth rattling, followed by a high fever. I assumed it was the Lyme disease flaring up, but she had never had symptoms like these before. I called Dr. L concerned. "Put her back on the antibiotics," she said and so we did.

That weekend was Father's Day. When I got home from church on Sunday I found Katherine shaking uncontrollably, white as a sheet with blue lips. It was over ninety degrees out and yet she looked like she had been bathing in ice water. Something was wrong. This felt different than the Lyme. John lived next door to us in the carriage house. He was like family and had helped raise Katherine since she was a toddler. I called him to come over. He took one look at her and we packed her in the car and headed to the emergency room.

We arrived at Kaiser's hospital and sat in the parking lot. Her symptoms seemed to have calmed down and I was not sure what to do. I had lost all trust in Kaiser. They had just pulled the plug on Jacob's nursing care. They had not helped in any way during her sickness. Even Dr. F, who "believed in Lyme" and approved her protocol, had tied hands for treatment and the best she offered Katherine was "make sure she has good nutrition and fresh air." They had failed us so deeply. Trust had been breeched. I was not sure what would happen if we took her into the hospital. There was such a strong denial of Lyme, such strangeness around this disease, that I was not sure it was safe for her. If the doctors would not consider her Lyme diagnosis, how could she get proper care? I imagined them pulling out her PICC line, leaving her unable to get future treatment.

The bottom line was I no longer trusted Kaiser. As we sat in the parking lot, assessing Katherine, we weighed our options and since her symptoms had subsided I decided to call an advice nurse. She asked a lot of questions and said if her symptoms came back to have her seen by urgent care. She did not think we needed to go to the emergency room. Relieved, we drove to a nearby coffee shop and ordered a pot of tea. I wanted to monitor her a bit longer before going home.

After two hours of abated symptoms, John and I drove her home and I tucked her into bed. "If you get sick in the night call me," I said to her with a kiss.

The next morning I discovered she had soaked the bed with sweat. She had been up all night with fever and was back to having the chills. It was now Monday and the Lyme clinic was open. I called Dr. L and she recommended a saline drip to hydrate Katherine. Sitting her on the couch, I made a make shift IV pole with a shower curtain hanger; hanging her drip from a picture frame.

John went to the store and bought a digital thermometer. It read 102 degrees. I did not know how unreliable digital thermometers could be. It was off, I would later find out. Her fever was much higher. Katherine continued to alternate between blue-lipped chills to soak-the-bed sweats. I did not know what to do. I did not know where to turn. I had called her Lyme doctor. I had called Kaiser. Something was wrong. I felt it, and yet she had been sick for so long. I assumed this was more of the Lyme.

I had never called my pastor for help before, but we needed prayers. I needed wisdom. I called his wife Sarah. "Something's wrong with Katherine." She could hear it in my voice.

"We're out on a bike ride, just a few blocks from Kaiser," she said, suggesting we take her to the emergency room and they meet us there.

I hung up the phone and took another look at Katherine. She needed to go. I called John. An urgency came over us. We wrapped her in blankets and threw her in the car. This was petal to the metal as John's old days as a taxi driver kicked in. He flew down Highway 12 to 101, holding Katherine's hand the entire way. It was a thirty minute drive door to door from our house to the hospital. She was slipping away. We could both see it. "Stay with us," he said, as her eyes rolled in and out of consciousness.

As he pulled up to the emergency room entrance, I jumped out of the car and ran inside, "There's something wrong with my daughter. We need help!" I called out. A nurse appeared and ran out the door. There was a long line winding from the check in desk. John was outside with Katherine collapsed in his arms. The entire emergency room stopped, all eyes on the scene unfolding.

"We need her Kaiser card," a woman emerged from behind a partition. I did not have it with me. John and the nurse appeared with Katherine in a wheel chair. She was delirious. "We need her Kaiser card," she said again. I rattled off her Kaiser number from memory. There was no time for protocol. The nurse who held the wheelchair took matters into her own hands and wheeled Katherine into the hospital, calling back the Kaiser number I had just recited.

"We need to x-ray her," a nurse said hastily ushering me out of the room. I went out to the waiting room where I found our pastor, Sarah and John waiting.

When they called me back in, she had been moved to a new room. I later found out it was the intensive care unit of the emergency room. "That's the same room Lilly was in," our pastor remarked before praying over Katherine.

A nurse came in. "She's in septic shock," she told us. Her fever had reached 106 degrees and her blood pressure dropped dangerously low. I watched her heart rate on the monitor. A nurse stood at her side in a constant vigil. Katherine extended her hand out. She was looking at it and talking about colors. Something was wrong, terribly wrong.

A story came to mind that a pastor once told our congregation years before. His father was in the hospital in critical condition and in marched his uncles, Bibles in hand. They said to the doctors, "You do what you are going to do. We'll do what we're going to do," and they began to pray.

I remembered my Bible study had an emergency prayer chain. I texted Katherine's vitals to our teaching leader and she sent out the prayer request to all the other Bible study leaders. As Katherine was in the emergency room, doctors and nurses trying to stabilize her, devoted Christian women were praying. A friend later told me when she read the prayer request she understood how serious it was and burst into tears. It brought her to her knees.

At the same time, one of the children's leaders showed her husband Katherine's vitals. He was a paramedic and said, "Her body is dying," as he walked out the door to work. Not long afterward he was helping a woman who had been in a car accident.

As she lay in a gurney going into the ambulance, she said to him, "I am a prayer warrior, is there anything you need prayer for? God always answers my prayers."

He remembered Katherine. "My wife's in a Bible study and there's a girl..."

You do what you are going to do doctors, and we'll do what we are going to do.

ELEVEN

Megan was the name of Katherine's nurse and she would not leave her side. John looked up sepsis on his iPad and his face fell. They decided not to tell me the details. There was nothing I could do but stand with my daughter and pray. The next day the doctors would tell me she had been thirty minutes from death. A half hour later and they would not have been able to stabilize her. Thirty minutes was the time it took to get from our house to the hospital, thirty minutes. I began to think of all the things that can happen in half an hour. She had been in and out of sepsis for days, unbeknownst to us, and it all came down to thirty minutes.

Sepsis is an infection of the blood and as it progresses it turns into septic shock. The heart pumps the infected blood through internal organs causing them to shut down and blood pressure to dramatically drop. The result is often organ failure and death. Katherine was in advanced stages of septic shock and they were doing their best to stabilize her. They wanted her transported to Oakland's PICU where they were better equipped to care for her, but they had to get her there. We were told to wait. They were putting together a team of pediatric specialists in Oakland to ride in the ambulance with her, in case any of her organs started shutting down on the way over.

I told my pastor that they should go home and get some rest. It was going to be a long night. They were hesitant to leave, but it was well past midnight and there was nothing more they could do. We just had to wait for the ambulance and I would ride over with Katherine. John would go home.

As Megan ended her shift, a new nurse signed in and looked over Katherine's chart. Megan was going on vacation and then transferring to Southern California. Katherine was her last patient at this hospital. As the incoming nurse reviewed her chart, she turned to Megan and said, "Good job, you saved a life tonight."

+ + +

Sackcloth and ashes. Old Testament mourning always included sackcloth and ashes. I never fully understood what that meant until the 10th floor. I could not bring myself to put on lipstick or do my hair. As long as Katherine lay in a hospital bed, I was going to live in sackcloth and ashes. No make up, no pretty clothes, just sackcloth and ashes.

Walking down Piedmont Avenue on coffee runs felt like culture shock. I watched people walk by oblivious to the 10th floor just a couple blocks away. Women wore bright colored dresses, I overheard someone complaining about their lunch and it all seemed so self-indulgent to me. I wanted to shake them and yell at them and tell them what vanity life is. I wanted them to know what really mattered. Everything became a transgression to me. There were two worlds now, the 10th floor and everywhere else. There was *suffering*. How could these people just carry on like nothing was happening, like my daughter was not a couple blocks away fighting for her life?

My world became black and white. The only place I wanted to be was by Katherine's side and every moment away was a body blow. I felt a physical ache in my heart when I was away from her for any length of time.

Sackcloth and ashes was the only response that made sense.

TWELVE

There was a rhythm to the 10th floor. Every morning the doctors, nutritionist, head nurse and social worker all made their rounds together in an intimidating herd of white coats moving through the PICU. We got moved to a room with a window where we could see sweeping views of Oakland. My friend Val came to visit and brought a little snow globe with a replica of the Eiffel Tower inside. When I shook it, glitter fell over Paris. I put it on the window ledge for Katherine to see, "Look Katherine, it's Paris in Oakland."

When Katherine was a little girl I took her to the De Young museum in San Francisco to see an Impressionist show. The paintings were on loan from the Musee d'Orsay in France and at the entrance of the exhibition there was a giant mural of 19th century Paris. I took Katherine's picture in front of the mural and whispered in her ear we were going to spend the day in France. We could not afford to travel, but we could pretend. And so we had a make-believe day in Paris, taking in a museum show followed by lunch at a café where I sipped cappuccino while she drank hot chocolate. She rolled her eyes at me as I continued our fantasy, but I shook my finger laughing, "One day you'll tell your kids how your mother took you to Paris." Later, we sat in the grass in Golden Gate Park. I made her a flower chain out of the little daisies that sprung up all over the ground and she wore it in her head like a wreath. She was my girl. Maybe we would never get to travel together, but we could have our version of Paris. I shook the snow globe and watched the glitter come down while looking out over the view of the bay.

+ + +

Katherine could not breathe. All night she struggled to catch her breath. I lay stretched out on the chair bed next to her, helpless to help her. Nurses came and went throughout the night, adjusting her oxygen levels. She could not lift her arms up from her side or sit without assistance. She had no strength. When they tried to get her to stand, she collapsed. She could not hold up her own body weight. During the day, doctors and nurses came by between visits with friends, who brought food, laughter and prayers.

When they were able to stabilize Katherine's breathing, they moved us out of the PICU to a room down the hall. We had been there for days and I had barely slept. Katherine begged me to go home to get some rest. The nurses suggested it too, and when John insisted, I knew that I had to listen. I did not want to be as far away as Sebastopol, so I booked a room at a nearby motel. It was a block from the hospital so I could be back at a moment's notice, but at least I would have a proper bed and my own shower. When I opened my motel room door, covering the wall beside the bed was a giant mural of Paris all lit up at night.

+ + +

I was worried that once Katherine was discharged from the hospital we would be left with no place to go for her health care. I begged the doctors to listen and make a plan. We could not go back to bedridden and no care. I had lost confidence in the Lyme clinic. They should have known the signs of sepsis and they did not. Kaiser had been no better, in fact worse, because they refused to treat her all along. We needed a plan, but they kept talking about dealing with the immediate crisis first. I thought the worst was over but, unknown to me, she was still in critical condition.

Dr. M was assigned as Katherine's hospital doctor. She said that while Katherine was in the hospital she would bring in pediatric specialists to evaluate her and promised to arrange a big interdisciplinary meeting with all of them before discharge. She assured me we would leave with a plan. From that point forward, there was an endless stream of specialists dropping by to evaluate Katherine and meet with us.

I was out on a lunch run when Infectious Disease came by. When I returned, I found a doctor sitting next to Katherine's bed talking to John who was visiting. Before I had a chance to say hello, she said to me, "We are never going to have a meeting of the minds." She was talking about Lyme disease.

I sat down next to her. At this point it still did not register who she was or what she was talking about. "We are not going to have a meeting of the minds?" I thought, "What was going on?" As we began to talk the pieces started to fit together. This was the infectious disease doctor I had talked to over a year ago, the doctor who said, "It is not Lyme disease. There is no other direction to go in. The mind does amazing things."

All the suffering Katherine had been through, the nightmare of the past year, could all be traced back to that comment, that refusal to consider Lyme disease, or any other possibility that Katherine's sickness was anything more than a figment of her imagination. As a result we were left on our own to sort out her medicine, costing us tens of thousands of dollars out of pocket, her bedridden and in constant pain, and ultimately resulting in where she was now, on the 10th floor, days out of the PICU.

My dear daughter lay next to us in a hospital bed. I looked this doctor in the eye. After all we had been through her response was, "We're not going to have a meeting of the minds." This was about Lyme disease to her. She did not know my mind. Other than that one conversation over a year ago, we had never spoken. She was so fixated on Lyme disease that she was unable to see the patient in front of her. My battle was over my daughter's health. I was not there to fight the Lyme fight. I was there to fight for Katherine.

Anger surged up through the inner most parts of me. It was a deep visceral reaction, a mother bear on her hind legs anger. I was looking into the face of the doctor who had been responsible for so much of my daughter's suffering. Pointing my finger at Katherine, but eyes fixed on the doctor, I said, *"You are responsible for this."*

A Holy Spirit fire was in my voice, *"From my lips to God's ears, you are responsible for this!"* Fire was now burning in my eyes. I could feel it and so could she. This was soul talk. She became agitated, standing in judgment, before me as a mother, but more so, her judgment was before the very throne of God. She was answerable for the suffering she caused my daughter, and it made her very uncomfortable. She jumped to her feet and scurried out of the room.

We had roommates, quiet roommates, who tenderly cared for their daughter. Concerned we had disturbed them, I poked my head around the curtain, "Sorry about that."

The mom was giddy. "Somebody had to say it!" she exclaimed, and pulled out her phone to show me pictures.

I wanted to turn my eyes away but I forced myself to look. She needed someone to see what happened to her daughter. Like us, she had taken her child to doctor after doctor, and she had been misdiagnosed. It turned out she had a rare condition that caused blistering all over her body, inside and out, like third-degree burns. The photographs were gruesome. It took everything in me to keep my eyes fixed on the screen. The blistering was so bad her daughter had to be put in a medically induced coma. I looked over at the young girl lying unaware of her surroundings in the hospital bed next to us. Her father sat patiently by her bed holding her hand. I could see the scars where the blisters had been all over her face and arms. Any part of her body that was exposed bore witness to these awful blisters. I offered to pray. Slipping my arm around her, we stood, two mothers on the 10th floor, praying for the healing of her daughter in the name of Jesus.

THIRTEEN

There is a janitor who prays for the children as she sweeps the floors of the PICU. "I like your earrings," I said, as she came into our room for the first time. They were hoops with crosses dangling off the ends.

"Thank you," she said, "*I just love Jesus.*" That was the beginning of our friendship. Later, when I was having one of my more difficult days, she stood and prayed with me, in the middle of the hallway, doctors, nurses and patients walking by. She held her broom in one hand and had her other arm around me. She did not care who heard, "IN THE NAME OF JESUS," she bellowed, her prayers echoing down the hall.

Once Katherine was out of the PICU and some of her strength returned, she could make hospital rounds and we walked the hallway loop. We ran into Lilly on one of our walks, and her face lit up like a Christmas tree, recognizing Katherine from church. She held out her little arm, "We have the same bracelets," she said to Katherine comparing. "You're sick too?" Lilly asked concerned. She was adorned from head to toe in Hello Kitty clothes, beaming her endless smile at us as she marveled over Katherine being there.

God was knitting something together. I could feel it. I did not want to waste one second of Katherine's suffering, and so I continued to pray for opportunities for God to use me.

+ + +

One morning on my way from my motel, I got a strong urge to pick up a box of coffee for the parents in the PICU. I remembered how much it meant to me on my first morning there. Not wanting to be gone too long, I decided to get it from the new hospital across the street. It turned out new hospital meant new café and new café meant new employees. The girls at the coffee shop had never put together a box of coffee before and it became clear that they had no idea what they were doing.

A long line was forming at the coffee counter. The girls were in over their heads and I was anxious to get back to Katherine. I checked the time. I had been there for nearly twenty minutes. Customers were growing inpatient. I was growing inpatient. Finally, frazzled, they handed me the box of coffee and I made my way to the 10th floor, set it down, poured myself a cup with plans to leave the rest for PICU parents, but I realized the box was only a quarter full. There was hardly anything left to share. "Whatever," I thought, "I'm going to see Katherine." All I wanted was to be with her. But then the urge came back. I needed to return this box and get a full one.

I knew that Holy Spirit voice. I had heard it so many times before. It was the still, quiet voice I heard when God was prompting me to do something. I wanted to swat it away like a fly. But it was persistent, and so, against my own will, my desire to be with my daughter, I reluctantly walked back to the coffee shop and asked for a refund. I could not wait for them to figure this out again and knew there was a Peet's coffee shop two blocks away. They were an established chain. Surely they would know how to fix a box of coffee.

Halfway there, I stopped in my tracks. I felt an inner tug of war. I was so tired, was I really even hearing a Holy Spirit prompting? Maybe this was just some dumb idea I thought up to get a box of coffee for the parents and had nothing to do with God. Maybe nobody up there even wanted coffee. I turned to make my way back to Katherine, but something stopped me. I stood on the sidewalk, halfway between the coffee shop and the hospital frozen in place. The thought persisted, "Go get the coffee." Ugh. Thankfully, Peet's had experienced employees who put it all together quickly. I practically ran back to the hospital. Just as I was setting the box down on the counter, a nurse poked her head out of PICU, "Oh good," she said, "a mom was just asking about coffee."

Moments later she was standing in front of me as I poured a cup of coffee for her. "Here," I said, as I held out the hot, steaming cup. I could feel Jesus in my arm as it extended to her.

Her son had brain cancer. He just had a tumor removed and he was recovering in the PICU. I understood the look on her face. I understood the fear in her voice. I felt her mother's heart and, as she drank her coffee, I listened.

FOURTEEN

John came to the hospital every evening. He worked long hours, but at night he would make the drive to Oakland to kiss Katherine good night and walk me to my motel room.

"There are wrongos here," he said looking around at all the seedy characters lingering about. He did not like me staying there, but there was no way I was going back to Sebastopol. I needed to be close to Katherine.

It was a shady place. I was woken up every night by what sounded like power washing. The first time I heard it, I thought it was morning and they were cleaning the sidewalk, but then I looked at the alarm clock and realized it was only 3 a.m. I was too tired to think much about it, but John said it sounded like a meth lab. Regardless of how seedy the motel may have been, I knew I would be okay. I felt God's covering, and somehow, looking up at that mural of the Eiffel Tower shimmering in the evening light, I felt God's presence. It was becoming an inside joke between us. It was God's way of saying, "I am here with you." It was His way of turning ashes into beauty, and it was personal. I imagined Katherine in her hospital room a block away. We both had our views of the Eiffel Tower as we went to sleep at night. I had put the snow globe on the window ledge of her room, so when she looked out, she too could see Paris in Oakland.

+ + +

The doctors told me to go home and pack my bags. Katherine was going to be in the hospital at least two more weeks, "If she gets out at all." She had been on antibiotics for so long that they were unable to find a match, they explained, it was all coming back resistant. Her vitals were under control, but the sepsis was not. "It is a virulent form of bacteria," they said.

"Do you mean deadly?" John asked.

"Yes."

We drove back to Sebastopol that night. John went to his house and I went to mine, but I could not sleep. It felt like someone had taken an ax and aimed straight for the center my chest. My world was dangerously out of control. In the car ride home John explained it all to me in more detail. If they could not find an antibiotic match then it was a matter of time before the sepsis started infecting her internal organs, and if that happened she would not come out alive. The doctors were preparing us for the worst.

I felt myself losing my grip on reality. Everything was spinning and the pressure of her illness, culminating in the PICU, was crashing down on me. Cracks were forming. I could not hold it together. Everything was out of control and I was not strong enough for this. Not for losing my daughter. I remembered hearing that when you are overcome with fear and worry to think about the worst-case scenario. I needed to pull myself together. "What was the worst thing that could happen?" I forced myself to think, "Katherine could die."

The worst thing that could happen was Katherine would die. "But if she did, she would be in heaven. She would be with Jesus." That was real. That was the truth. It was the unbendable reality I was facing and I felt the sharpest, clearest moment of faith I had ever had. Everything else was out of focus, but the reality of Jesus and heaven was clear. All of a sudden, a peace washed over me. It was a millisecond of peace and purity of faith, but it was all I needed to regain clarity. From that point on I could pray.

> *"Truly I tell you, if you have faith as small as a mustard seed, you can say to this mountain, 'Move from here to there,' and it will move. Nothing will be impossible for you."* (Matthew 17:20)

"Katherine is a Christian girl," I thought, "it is impossible for her to die from an infection in her blood." This was the powers and principalities of this world. Now, instead of being broken and weak, I was strong. I was a prayer warrior for my daughter and this was a life or death battle. *The devil was not going to take my daughter through her blood. It was impossible.* This was a spiritual battle that had already been won by Jesus' blood on the cross. Right then and there, I prayed for Jesus to replace Katherine's blood with His blood.

+ + +

I could not get back to the hospital fast enough Saturday morning. I had been up all night praying. The faith I felt so clearly in the middle of the night had been replaced by a dull ache by the light of day. I just wanted to be back with my daughter. The 10th floor and Oakland seemed so far away. We had at least an hour's drive ahead of us and I wanted to make a quick stop on the way to pick up balloons. I needed to brighten her room with something cheerful and they did not allow flowers in the pediatric ward.

I ran into Safeway a crazy woman. All my Christianity went out the window as I demanded a perfect bouquet of balloons from the poor sales clerk. Nothing was right. They only had the regular size "get well" balloons, I wanted a great big one, but I did not want to waste time. I just wanted to get back to Oakland. In the car I had a melt down about how ugly her balloons were. Everything about them was wrong from the color combination to the ribbons. I complained to poor John who listened patiently. I just wanted something beautiful for Katherine. "Why is life so unfair?" I demanded, grumbling about the balloons all the way to the hospital.

I had barely stepped out of the elevator doors when a nurse came rushing toward me. "Where did you get those?" she was anxious to know. The gift shop had closed due to the hospital move and the new one had not opened yet. Parents were asking where they could get something to brighten their children's rooms.

I brought the bouquet to show Katherine and we laughed. It truly was a terrible combination of colors, but they were perfect to hand out individually to the other children in the hospital. I had been so worked up about a bunch of balloons and all along God had a better plan. Katherine did not need a dozen balloons. She only needed one to add a little cheer to her room. I pulled out the special one, the acrylic balloon that had flowers printed on it and read "get well," and gave it to her and then made my way down the hall handing out the rest of the balloons to children in hospital beds as tired parents looked at me gratefully.

+ + +

The neurologist was the last specialist to visit Katherine's room. I was exhausted from staying up praying and the faith I had in the middle of the night was now wavering back to the fear of losing my daughter. I was too tired to care what she was saying. She seemed to drone on and on and I just wanted her to go away. I tilted my chair back. I could barely stand another word. I leaned my head back against the widow ledge and all of a sudden a loud "CRACK" sounded off like gunfire. Everyone jumped back. I leapt out of my chair. It was Paris in Oakland. I had hit the snow globe with the back of my head and it lay shattered, bits of glass mixed with glitter and sticky goo spread across the floor. "I'll take care of it," I volunteered, needing to get out of the room.

I stopped at the nursing station to ask about cleaning supplies, but before I could get the words out I saw Sarah. She was visiting with Beth and Lilly and the sight of her was too much to take in. I was overwhelmed by her warmth and love and as she wrapped me in a big hug, I broke down trying to explain everything that was going on. She looked me in the eye and said, "She's going to be okay."

I was so tired. "I have faith. Let me have faith for you," she said, and just like that, she lifted my burden and I could breathe again.

FIFTEEN

Sunday morning while our church band was playing, while worship songs were being sung, prayers prayed and the Word of God preached, we got the news Katherine was healed. They had tested her blood three times on Saturday and the sepsis was gone. I had prayed for Jesus to replace Katherine's blood with His blood, and just like that, victory. She was healed. But not only the sepsis, her Lyme symptoms had disappeared too.

It was a get up and walk Bible story being lived out on the 10th floor of Kaiser's Oakland hospital, and my daughter was a living, breathing testimony to the power of Jesus and prayer.

First stop, Lilly and Beth, as I shared the miraculous news of the morning. She told me that Lilly had slept through the night with no seizures. We rejoiced and prayed and thanked God. Beth said, "One day, we'll both stand up on the altar at church and praise God for what He has done for our girls." Everyone I saw that day, I told about the miracle of Jesus and how He healed my daughter.

As Katherine and I were walking the hospital loop, a nurse poked her head out of the PICU and could not believe she was the same girl she had cared for. Her eyes brimmed up with tears as she recalled how sick Katherine had been, "If only all the children turned out like this," she said. The same child who did not have the strength to lift her arms or ability to breathe on her own was now walking the halls healed. All the doctors we had been to, all the specialists, all the years of pain and suffering, all gone. Just like that.

Her doctors wanted her treated for two weeks with powerful IV antibiotics. "It kills everything," they said, wanting to take no chances.

If there was any residual Lyme or sepsis, God could use this medicine to finish His healing work. I remembered my pastor's sermon, "You do your medicine and we'll do ours."

+ + +

The hospital was clearing out floor by floor as patients were transferred across the street to the new building, but the 10th floor was the last to go.

We had a Nigerian nurse named Daisy who told jokes and taught us African dance moves as we made our way around the hospital loop. Katherine was getting better. Dr. M told us they were moving up the meeting with the specialists. They wanted to do it before the big move, and then we would be transferred to Santa Rosa to complete her IV antibiotic treatment.

As we made our way around the 10th floor, Katherine and I ran into the mom I had given the cup of coffee to and she invited us into the PICU to see her son. We went back through to the other side of those dreaded doors and watched as her son lay peacefully asleep, head bandaged, giant tumor recently removed. I knew the look on her face and offered to pray for her son. She gave a nod of agreement. As I reached my arm around her to pray, she backed away, "No, no. I can't," she protested.

"You don't have to," I said, "I'll pray for you," and

once again I felt Jesus moving through me as I put my arm around her and prayed for her son.

There was another woman sitting with the boy, his other mom. They were a couple, and here in the PICU, on the 10th floor of Kaiser's hospital, a lesbian couple and two Christians prayed over a sick child in the name of Jesus.

Later that day, when I went out for a lunch run, I saw a stuffed animal in a window, a soft little lamb. I bought it for the boy. His mom had mentioned he loved animals and somehow it had reminded me of him, looking so sweet and vulnerable in his hospital bed. It did not even occur to me at the time, it was a lamb. *The lamb of God. Jesus.*

+ + +

It came time for the much-anticipated meeting with all of the specialists. John took time off work to be there. The social worker arrived early, but none of the specialists showed up. Dr. M came to Katherine's hospital room to tell us they were not coming. The meeting had been canceled. There was no exit plan. We were being transferred to Santa Rosa that evening to finish her treatment there.

I knew God had healed her sepsis. We had evidence that was under control. They were able to monitor it in the lab. She had the Jesus blood transfusion. But there was no conclusive test for her Lyme disease. She had been so sick for so long. What if her symptoms came back? Once again I felt a Kaiser blow. "How could none of the specialists show up?"

We were transferred to Santa Rosa that night. The next day the 10th floor was moving to the new hospital. I could not get out of there fast enough.

As Katherine rode in the ambulance to Santa Rosa, John and I followed behind. This time we were crossing the bridge the other way, toward home.

+ + +

Katherine was given a private room in the maternity ward in the Santa Rosa hospital. It felt luxurious after what we had been through. No patients separated by thin curtains, no scars from blisters or children clinging to life. The look of worried parents was replaced by smiles of proud mothers walking the halls with their newborn babies. Katherine and I stopped and admired them as they went by.

Katherine spent a week in the Santa Rosa hospital. Our pastor stopped by for a visit one day and said she looked like a different kid. The veil of pain that had covered her face for so long was gone. On the wall was a pain chart with different facial expressions. I recognized six to eight as the expression she wore for so many years. The doctors had been wrong for so long. They had all failed us. All the years her pain was dismissed, the insistence she was depressed, the minimizing, dismissing and denial of care. In the end, the pictures on the pain scale said it all. And now the pain was gone. She had a new expression on her face and brightness in her eyes.

Finally the day arrived for her to be discharged. For the first time in weeks I put on a pretty dress and make up. Instead of pulling my hair back in a ponytail I wore it down. No more sackcloth and ashes. My girl was coming home.

SIXTEEN

Not everybody gets the miracle. Some God heals and others He does not. Katherine and Lilly were both released on the same day from the 10th floor, but as Katherine got better, Lilly got worse. She was diagnosed with a rare form of brain cancer.

By Christmas she had gone home to be with the Lord. All the faith God had built up through Katherine's illness was shattered by the death of Lilly. I felt lost and angry at God and in my anger, darkness settled in that I had never felt before. "This is what it feels like to be separated from God," I thought, and yet I was the one who had done the separating.

After all God had done, I was angry at Him for taking Lilly, and confused. I did not understand. She was only five years old and one of the sweetest little five year olds I had ever met. Always with a smile, always adorned in bright colors, pinks, yellows and Hello Kitty clothes, she was a bright spot in a dark world. Why did God take Lilly but spare Katherine? That haunted me. They had both been in the same bed in the emergency room. We were on the 10th floor at the same time and discharged on the same day. Our stories were intertwined and none of it made any sense. How could I rejoice in Katherine's miracle in light of Lilly's death? I felt guilty I had my child while Beth lost hers. "Why God?" was all I could get out in prayer.

"Trust in the Lord with all your heart and lean not on your own understanding; in all your ways submit to

Him, and He will make your paths straight."
(Proverbs 3:5-6)

Every time I thought "Why?" That passage came to mind, over and over again, *"Trust in the Lord with all your heart and lean not on your own understanding..."* That was His answer to me. It was not mine to understand. It was only my job to trust God has His reasons and I do not get to be privy to all of them.

Beth has her story to tell of a mother's heart and I have mine. If I had any say in the matter, things would have turned out differently.

God knit something powerful together on the 10th floor. He had a work to do and I do not understand it all. Some colors in this tapestry seem too dark to comprehend and others shine brightly, but the picture is not finished. He is still using both Lilly and Katherine's stories, and one day Beth and I will stand on an altar, even greater than the one at church; we will stand before the very throne of God, and maybe then He will show us the whole picture, and maybe then I will understand.

SEVENTEEN

Moses never got to enter the Promised Land. Instead, God took him to a mountain top and showed Him the land the Israelites would inhabit, but he would never go in. He went somewhere better. Moses walked into the presence of the Lord and entered into heaven.

God is the God of miracles. He came down into the world in a human form and bore the consequences of our sins on the cross, shed His blood on our behalf and took the penalty upon Himself. *"By His stripes we are healed"* (Isaiah 53:5).

By His blood He healed the body of Katherine. But even greater than that is the salvation healing of the human soul that happens every day when people give their lives over to Jesus and accept His promise of eternal life.

Katherine is flesh-and-blood testimony to His power and grace. I too am testimony to His saving grace, cleansed from my sins and made new by the blood of Christ. Anyone who calls on the name of Jesus as Lord and believes it in their heart (Romans 10:9-10) can have the miracle of Christ's blood and new life breathed into them, and that is bigger, far bigger than anything that happened on the 10th floor. That is salvation.

God is good and His ways are not our ways. Those weeks of darkness I felt over Lilly's death were like a shadow of what it must feel like to enter into eternal darkness, separated from the Love of God, not because of Him, but because I pulled away.

EPILOGUE

It has been over a year since the hospital and Katherine's headaches and debilitating pain never returned. She is thriving, attending school and planning for her future. We go back to Oakland every Saturday to see a Christian acupuncturist. She has some residual effects from long-term infection that we are treating naturally.

While she is in her appointment, I walk down Grand Avenue, past the Grand Lake Theatre to Lake Merrit, where there is an old woman who sweeps the city sidewalks. I see her every week as I walk around the lake. I put on a grey sweatshirt and sunglasses, camouflaged into the city as I people watch. There are old men who sit on benches watching the water and young couples who lay on the grassy banks and kiss. Families gather with barbeques and have big parties playing loud music. I often pass a circus school whose students tie ropes between trees as they attempt balancing acts. I make my way around the lake, hearing languages from every nation, eavesdropping on conversations when I can. Life is being lived out around the lake. Life is being lived out in Oakland and I come to make my peace with it.

Tall buildings loom in the distance and I know not far from where I stand, are the two parallel hospitals. The 10th floor is now empty, awaiting demolition. I imagine the new hospital across the street, with its pediatric floor where mothers are standing over children wondering if they are coming home.

I say a prayer. There is too much grief in the world. I watch the woman sweep the city sidewalk and I understand. I am that woman too, sweeping the grief and pain and dirt and grit from my heart with each step. God is at work. God is at work in every step, in every sweep, in every day. He is there.

"Could we with ink the ocean fill
And were the skies of parchment made,
Were every stalk on earth a quill
And every man a scribe by trade;
To write the love of God above
Would drain the oceans dry;
Nor could the scroll contain the whole
Though stretched from sky to sky."

-The Love of God

ACKNOWLEDGEMENTS

First and foremost, all praise, honor and glory to God.

Thank you, Katie Wilson, for your graphic design skills, Katherine Coviello, for help with the cover design, technical details and editing of *Paris in Oakland,* and to Kelly Holt Ph.D. and Pastor Adam Wilson for your sharp eyes in proofreading.

For all the people who helped us through Katherine's illness, we remain deeply grateful. Thank you to John, for your dedication to our family and for your godly example. To our church, Calvary the Rock, thank you for all the prayers, visits and meals. Special thanks to Pastor Ross and Barb, Pastor Adam, Katie and the youth group, Women to Women, and our faithful neighbors Allison, Dillon, Gloria, Tom, and Sharline-you helped stitch together so much more than a dress.

Thursday morning prayer group, words cannot express the gratitude I feel toward each of you: Robin A., Robin H., Robin M., Lisa and Tricia, thank you for helping with the heavy lifting. Wednesday morning B.S.F., I am eternally grateful for your prayers and support, with special thanks to Diedre, Margie and Kimberly, and to my lunchtime posse (and chocolate cake cohorts), Elizabeth, Christina, Julie and Pippa.

Darcy, you are not only a great stylist, but you and Lou blessed our home so much, thank you. To our Sebastopol family, the Qu's, the girls got to witness a miracle, and to Karen and Jen P., we are grateful for your help and prayers, especially with Katherine's schooling.

Thank you to my family for your love and support, with special thanks to Mom, Dad, Cynthia, Aunt Diane, Aunt Linda and cousin Chris. To everyone who delivered a meal, visited, prayed or said an encouraging word, thank you. Each of you helped carry us through the dark days of Lyme disease.

We remain grateful to all the doctors and nurses who went above and beyond with Katherine's healthcare: Dr. A., Dr. Shi, nurse Israel, Megan, the wonderful nurses at Oakland's PICU, as well as the grants and foundations that made her treatment possible: Clinic of Angels, LymeLight Foundation, Lyme Aid 4 Kids, and Lyme-TAP.

A very special thank you to Jen V. for bringing Paris to Oakland.

REFERENCES

1. *The Song of Bernadette*, movie written by George Seaton; directed by Henry King (1943), adapted by Franz Werfel's 1941 novel, *The Song of Bernadette.*

2. Bible quotes from the New International Version, Zondervan Press, 2011

3. L.B. Cowman, edited by Jim Reimann, *Streams in the Dessert,* (Michigan: Zondervan Press, 1997), page 99

4. John Bunyan, *The Pilgrim's Progress*

5. *The Love of God*, a hymn by Frederick M. Lehman, 1917

RESOURCES

Bible Study: To find a Bible study near you, visit www.bsfinternational.org. Bible Study Fellowship International has 1,000 classes in 39 countries around the world.

Lyme Disease: For more about information Lyme disease go to www.ilads.org or www.lymedisease.org

31012517R10066

Made in the USA
Middletown, DE
15 April 2016